Let's Make

Cake Pops

by Mari Bolte

NORWOOD HOUSE 🏠 PRESS

Norwood House Press

For information regarding Norwood House Press, please visit our website at: www.norwoodhousepress.com or call 866-565-2900.

PHOTO CREDITS: page 4: ©vm / Getty Images; page 7: ©DenisProduction.com / Shutterstock; page 8: ©Witsanu Thangsombat / EyeEm / Getty Images; page 11: ©Raimunda-Iosantos / Shutterstock; page 12: ©Ahanov Michael / Shutterstock; page 14: ©AnnaKalinicheva / Shutterstock; page 17: ©Arina P Habich / Shutterstock; page 19: ©Rosa Herrara; page 21: ©Rosa Herrara ; page 22: ©Rosa Herrara; page 23: ©Rosa Herrara; page 24: ©Rosa Herrara ; page 27: ©Rosa Herrara; page 28: ©Rosa Herrara / Shutterstock

Hardcover ISBN: 978-1-68450-777-1
Paperback ISBN: 978-1-68404-754-3

LIBRARY OF CONGRESS CATALOGING-IN-PUBLICATION DATA
Library of Congress Cataloging-in-Publication Data has been filed and is available at catalog.loc.gov

353N—082022
Manufactured in the United States of America in North Mankato, Minnesota.

Contents

CHAPTER 1

Cake pops can come in any color imaginable.

All about Cake Pops

There's nothing more delicious than a big slice of cake. Light, airy cake and sweet, colorful frosting—what's not to love? But sometimes, you might only want a little bit.

Cake pops let you have a small taste. Cake pops are cake and frosting rolled together. Then, they are dipped in colorful **candy melts**. A lollipop stick makes them easy to eat in just a bite or two!

People have been eating cakes for thousands of years! Ancient people did not have cake pans or **molds** like we do today. Their cakes were shaped into balls before being baked over a fire.

Cupcakes were first made in the late 1700s. They were baked in small dishes or cups. Some people called these little cakes "number cakes."

Baking got faster and easier when the first boxed cake mix was sold in 1933. With just water, a gingerbread cake could be made quickly. By the mid-1940s, there were many types of boxed cake mix on the market.

Cakes come in an almost endless variety of flavors. Chocolate, vanilla, and funfetti are three of the most popular.

Hostess sold the first cupcakes to shoppers in 1919, but the little cakes didn't get frosting until the 1950s. Buttercream frosting came out around the same time. It's a mixture of sugar, butter, cream, and a flavor, like vanilla or almond.

Bakerella has inspired people around the world to create their own unique cake pops.

Angie Dudley, also known as Bakerella, made the first cake pops in 2008. She was a **blogger**. First, she posted a recipe for red velvet cake balls. She had eaten them at a party and asked the baker how to make them.

The recipe started with one box of red velvet cake mix. The baked cake was crumbled and combined with half a can of cream cheese frosting. Next, the cake balls were dipped in chocolate candy melts.

Then, Bakerella took the recipe one step further. She pierced the cake balls with lollipop sticks and stuck them in a foam block to dry. She called them cakesicles and cake pops. They were an instant success.

From there, Bakerella learned how to make her cake pops into adorable shapes, from sharks to boxes of popcorn to cartoon characters. She published a book about cake pops that was a best-seller for weeks. Her cake pops were cute and easy to make, and she shared how to do it with everyone.

People love cake pops because they can be made in an endless variety of flavors. Plain white or chocolate cake can be flavored with chocolate, raspberry, or even peanut butter frosting.

People on special diets can also enjoy cake pops. Gluten-free and vegan cake mixes make it possible. Allergy-friendly and low-sugar mixes are out there too. Any kind of cake and any flavor of frosting can become a cake pop!

Cake pops are sold individually or in **bouquets**. They can be made to look like miniature versions of real foods, animals, or anything a baker can imagine. No matter what the holiday or event, there's a way to make a cake pop that matches! They are perfect for gifts, party favors, or just for fun.

Parts of a Cake Pop

Toppings

Crumbled cake & frosting

Candy melt

Lollipop stick

The inside of cake and bread is called the crumb.

CHAPTER 2

Make Your Own Cake Pops

Cake has flour, sugar, baking soda or baking powder, fat like butter or oil, liquid, and eggs. Each plays an important role. Wheat flour has protein. When the **protein** is combined with water, it creates **gluten**. Gluten is stretchy. It gives baked goods strength and elasticity. Gluten-free mixes use potato or corn starches or xanthan gum instead. Xanthan gum is a food additive made from a sweetener.

The frosting in cake pops is the same frosting that is often used to decorate cakes and cupcakes.

Baking soda or powder helps cake rise. When combined with an **acidic** ingredient, they produce a gas called carbon dioxide. Lemon juice, buttermilk, and chocolate are all acids. When mixed, these ingredients create a bubbly foam. The foam inflates the stretchy gluten, creating air pockets. This process gives cake a light and airy texture.

Sugar makes the cake sweet. With water, sugar locks in moisture. It also prevents gluten from developing as fast. This is why cake stays moist for a long time.

When cooked or baked, sugar undergoes **caramelization**. This means it gets a deep, nutty flavor. Caramelization also helps baked goods turn brown in the oven.

Fats like oil or butter add moisture, color, and flavor to cake. Whipping softened butter and sugar together is a technique called creaming. The sugar is evenly mixed into the butter. Sugar molecules cut into the butter, leaving the mixture light and fluffy. It makes more air pockets for baking powder or soda. Fats also weaken gluten so the cake does not get too chewy.

Candy melts are a sweet candy coating. They are sold at grocery and craft stores. Candy melts are mostly sugar and oil. This means they melt easily—and taste good!

Candy melts can be easily melted in the microwave for dipping or drizzling. If your candy melts come out too thick, you can thin the mixture with oil. Using water would cause the mixture to **seize**. The same thing would happen when thinning melted chocolate.

Both candy melts and chocolate are made of fats, like vegetable oil and cocoa butter, and dry particles like cocoa powder and sugar. Water and oils don't mix! Water moistens the dry particles, which clump and get grainy. Food coloring is water-based. So, it is best to buy candy melts that are already colored.

Candy melts are sold near baking supplies and ingredients. They are also called candy coatings and confectionery wafers.

Candy melts

Sprinkles

Chocolate chips

There are many tips and tricks for making the best cake pops! Making sure you use the right amount of cake to frosting is the first step. If there is too much frosting, the cake ball won't stay together. Add just enough frosting to make the cake a little moist. Start with a little frosting and add more until the mixture holds its shape when squeezed.

Don't make your pops too big, or they might fall right off the stick. Dipping the lollipop stick into candy melts before pushing it into a cake ball is helpful too. The candy melts act like glue. Once the candy melts harden on the lollipop stick, you can then dip the whole cake pop.

Start with a small quantity of candy melts. You can always melt more. If the melts get too cool, you will have to heat them again. Too-cool melts can also make your cake pops lumpy.

Materials Checklist

- ✓ boxed cake mix and required ingredients
- ✓ mixing bowl
- ✓ mixing spoon
- ✓ buttercream frosting
- ✓ plate or baking sheet

- ✓ candy melts
- ✓ lollipop sticks
- ✓ decorations, such as sprinkles or more candy melts
- ✓ foam block or tall water glass filled with rice or beans

Be sure you don't over-mix the cake batter. This prevents extra gluten from forming, keeping the crumb soft.

CHAPTER 3

In the Kitchen!

Now that you know what goes into making cake pops, it's time to make your own! First you will bake the cake, then mix in the frosting. Next you will form balls and dip in melted candy. Here are the steps:

1. With an adult's help, bake a cake following the instructions on the boxed cake mix.

2. Let the cake cool completely. Then, crumble the cake into small pieces in the mixing bowl.

Add frosting a little bit at a time. You can always add more, but you can't remove any once it's been mixed in.

3. Add about 1/2 cup of frosting to the cake crumbs. Mix until well combined. The mixture should be just moist enough to stick together.

4. Gently roll into cake balls. They can be as small as 1 tablespoon or as large as 3 tablespoons. Set them on a plate or baking sheet, making sure they do not touch. Chill for 2 hours.

5. With an adult's help, prepare the candy melts according to the package instructions.

6. Dip the end of a stick into the candy melts. Then, press the stick into a cake ball. Repeat until all the cake pops have sticks. Chill for 10 minutes.

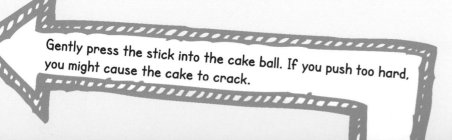

Gently press the stick into the cake ball. If you push too hard, you might cause the cake to crack.

7. Reheat the candy melts if needed. Dip a cake pop into the candy melts. Tap the stick on the side of the bowl to remove any excess.

8. Decorate the cake pop while the candy melts are still wet.

Letting extra candy melts drip off keeps your cake pop from getting too heavy.

9. Push the end of the cake pop into the foam block or tall water glass filled with rice or beans, or set it on a baking sheet. Decorate the rest of the cake pops.

10. Chill for 10 to 15 minutes. Your cake pops are now ready to eat!

All of the ingredients, and your creativity, have worked together to create these special cake pops. Enjoy!

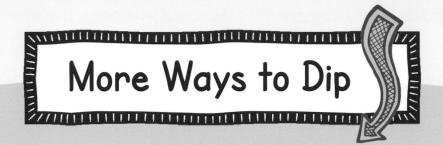

More Ways to Dip

Congratulations! You have made cake pops. Now see if there are ways to make them even better. Use any of these changes and see how they improve your cake pops.

- Skip step 8. Then, after the coating is set, drizzle a different colored candy melt over the cake pops. Decorate with sprinkles. The sprinkles will only stick to the wet drizzle!

- Try different and interesting flavor combinations of cake and frosting.

- When shaping the cake balls, try pinching the dough into shapes to create animals or characters.

Can you think of any ways you could improve or change your cake pops to make them better?

Glossary

acidic (uh-sid-IK): containing acid, a chemical with a sharp taste

blogger (BLOG-uhr): a person who writes for an online journal or website

bouquets (boh-KAYS): groups of flowers or other objects arranged into a bunch

candy melts (KAN-dee MELTS): wafers of candy that melt and re-harden into a sweet coating

caramelization (kayr-mel-ize-ay-SHUN): the process of browning sugars by adding heat

gluten (GLOO-ten): a protein found naturally in grains, such as wheat

molds (MOLDS): hollow containers used to give shape to something

protein (PROH-teen): a part of certain foods, such as wheat, meat, and dairy products, that is important for healthy growth

seize (SEEZ): turns into a solid lump or paste

For More Information

Books

Eboch, M. M. *Delectable Cupcakes with a Side of Science: An Augmented Recipe Science Experience.* North Mankato, MN: Capstone Press, 2019.

Goldman, Duff. *Super Good Baking for Kids.* New York, NY: Harper, 2020.

Tosi, Christina. *Milk Bar: Kids Only.* New York, NY: Clarkson Potter, 2020.

Websites

Bakerella (https://www.bakerella.com) The official blog of Bakerella.

Baketivity (https://baketivity.com/your-guide-to-cake-pops/) A guide to cake pop history, tutorials, and tips.

Wilton (https://blog.wilton.com/how-to-make-cake-pops-easy-cake-pop-recipe/) Wilton's guide to making the perfect cake pop.

Index

About the Author

Mari Bolte has worked in publishing as a writer and editor for more than 15 years. She has written dozens of books about things like science and craft projects, historical figures and events, and pop culture. She lives in Minnesota.